Misty Copeland

CHERRY LAKE PRESS

Published in the United States of America by Cherry Lake Publishing
Ann Arbor, Michigan
www.cherrylakepublishing.com

Reading Adviser: Marla Conn, MS, Ed., Literacy specialist, Read-Ability, Inc.
Book Designer: Jennifer Wahi
Illustrator: Jeff Bane

Photo Credits: ©Rigucci/Shutterstock, 5; ©Best Photos by Anna Paul/Shutterstock, 7; Courtesy of Under Armour, 9; ©Naim Chidiac, Abu Dhabi Festival/Gilda N. Squire/Wikimedia, 11, 22; ©lev radin/Shutterstock, 13; Courtesy of MindLeaps, 15, 17, 19, 23; ©Featureflash Photo Agency/Shutterstock, 21; Jeff bane, cover, 1, 6, 8, 14

Library of Congress Cataloging-in-Publication Data

Names: Sarantou, Katlin, author. | Bane, Jeff, 1957- illustrator.
Title: Misty Copeland / [author: Katlin Sarantou ; illustrator: Jeff Bane].

Description: Ann Arbor, Michigan : Cherry Lake Publishing, [2020] | Series: My itty-bitty bio | Includes index. | Audience: Grades: K-1 | Summary: "The My Itty-Bitty Bio series are biographies for the earliest readers. This book examines the life of Misty Copeland in a simple, age-appropriate way that will help children develop word recognition and reading skills. Includes a table of contents, author biography, timeline, glossary, index, and other informative backmatter"-- Provided by publisher.
Identifiers: LCCN 2019034650 (print) | LCCN 2019034651 (ebook) | ISBN 9781534158757 (hardcover) | ISBN 9781534161054 (paperback) | ISBN 9781534159907 (pdf) | ISBN 9781534162204 (ebook)
Subjects: LCSH: Copeland, Misty--Juvenile literature. | African American ballerinas--Biography--Juvenile literature.
Classification: LCC GV1785.C635 S33 2020 (print) | LCC GV1785.C635 (ebook) | DDC 792.802/8092 [B]--dc23
LC record available at https://lccn.loc.gov/2019034650
LC ebook record available at https://lccn.loc.gov/2019034651

Printed in the United States of America
Corporate Graphics

About the author: Katlin Sarantou grew up in the cornfields of Ohio. She enjoys reading and dreaming of faraway places.

About the illustrator: Jeff Bane and his two business partners own a studio along the American River in Folsom, California, home of the 1849 Gold Rush. When Jeff's not sketching or illustrating for clients, he's either swimming or kayaking in the river to relax.

I was born in 1982. I grew up in California.

My family didn't have a lot of money.

I started dancing when I was 13.
I took **ballet** classes.

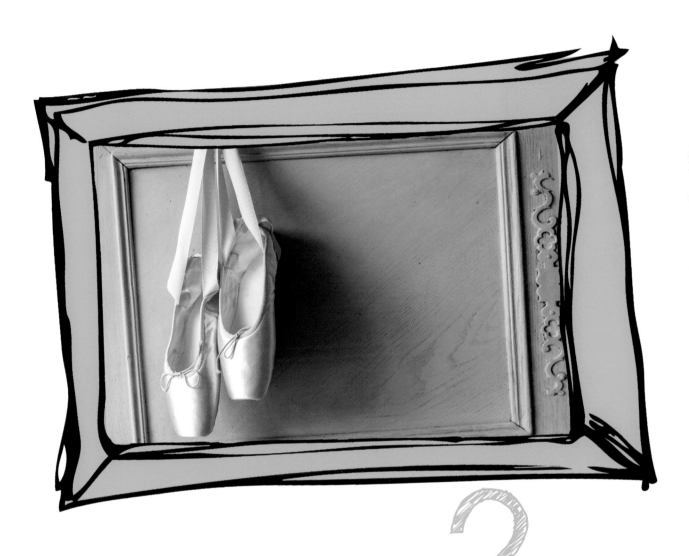

What do you like to do?

I won my first award at 15. I got **scholarships** for dance.

I joined the **American Ballet Theatre**.

I became **principal dancer**.

I was the first African American woman to do this.

I have received many awards for dancing.

I was one of the top 100 most **influential** people in the world.

I love dancing. I also love giving back. I give back to kids in need.

In what ways do you help others?

I worked with MindLeaps. The organization teaches dance to kids in Rwanda. This is a country in Africa.

Dance teaches important life skills.

I started a girls' program with MindLeaps. I also started a scholarship.

I hope to **inspire** girls. I hope they never give up on their dreams.

What would you like to ask me?

2015

1980

Born
1982

2015

2080

glossary

American Ballet Theatre (uh-MER-ih-kuhn bah-LAY THEE-uh-tur) a famous ballet company based in New York City

ballet (bah-LAY) a style of dance that uses exact and graceful movements

influential (in-floo-EN-shuhl) having the power to change or affect someone or something

inspire (in-SPIRE) to fill someone with a feeling or idea

principal dancer (PRIN-suh-puhl DAN-sur) the main or most important dancer in a dance company

scholarships (SKAH-lur-ships) money given to people to help pay for school

index

24